Extraction

Enquiries should be made to Ralph Wessman, Walleah Press, 23 Hobart Road, South Launceston, Tasmania 7249.

Extraction

Kim Nielsen-Creeley

ISBN 9780645797725

Cover by Kim Nielsen-Creeley
Title: 'Maps' (section of drawing, graphite and Pitt pastel)

Typset in Utsaah 13.5 pt
Printed by IngramSpark

Extraction

Kim Nielsen-Creeley

contents

For my daughter and granddaughter Veronica Rose Creeley, and Vera May Arnold.

Kim Nielsen-Creeley

Kim was born in Queenstown, a mining town in lutruwita/Tasmania. Her poetry has a keen sense of place, responding to landscape and history. She has an honours degree in fine art, and has recently incorporated poetry beneath the surface of her work.

This is her first full collection of poetry.

dancing in dirt

see humanity's relationship
with dirt and germs
the matter out of place
now we are all unclean
that March I went to bed for months
swathed in an archaic foment

I did like standing at the front at gigs
feeling grooves with moves
skin and breath discharging
negotiating close space
shedding
voiding lost sweat

by October from the pulp
fermenting in microbial sludge
rhythm returned with a soft lead pencil
on new lined paper

girt

a book of maps

A Continent Takes Shape the title states
as if it didn't have shape or purpose or exist
before the Dutch, the French or Cook

starting earlier with missing bits
the cartographers eye, from seaward
traced edges without an interior
and imagined other unseen things

p 71, Sullivan's Cove charted in 1831
black lines, after the fact, interrogated intrusions
illusions of grey, from the broken nature of marks
on edges, unreal tides sweeping back the project

streets colonised by Campbell, Macquarie
Collins, Davey, Argyle, Liverpool and Murray
et al., the patriarchal foundation
so absolutely added, a jetty jutting out

another one proposed, off a lumber yard
filling up the land, on the left
superior large allotments
for Captain Haig, Mr Hamilton
Captain Kelly, Captain Reid, Mr Grant
they could be in the burial ground now
as parkland — the key is clear
government, private and proposed
over-looking unnamed ½ and ¼ acre blocks

Argyle Street, above Collins, shows the bridge
crossing the Rivulet, the reason this city exists
despite the typhoid. my mind has wandered off
like the water course, already diverted further down
a diversion waiting for another, then another deluge

A Continent Takes Shape, Egon & Elsie Kunz
Ref: Hobart Rivulet

barometers, tracks, maps, prospects, and a dog called Fly

Notes re-ordered from the journals of the track maker, prospector, plant collector and explorer Thomas Bather Moore (1850-1919) held at the Tasmanian Museum and Art Gallery

glass falling

very wet

wet & windy

wet day at camp

very wet, all day

a nasty wet day

heavy rain & hail

heavy showers all day

heavy storm all day

heavy rain and sleet, showers all day

showery all day, scrub very wet

showery morning & rain towards evening

very heavy rain, snow & hail squalls

wet

ducks, swans, platypus

crawfish, lobster, eels

two badgers in snares

we found potatoes growing there

Fly got two wombats
Fly got a kangaroo
Fly got a kangaroo
Fly got a very large kangaroo

lines drawn, degrees recorded
records mailed, a good letter from home
daily journals, letters, wires, meetings
goods arrived safely. got all camp requisites
our path is chosen, we cannot complain

men packing, set men to work
men went for loads
lodes of potential
pegging the intervening lines
pegged down spur. potential profitable reefs
iron dykes in a matrix. outcrops prospected

moss & ferns for the Baron & the Royal Society
button grass ignited, smoke
six snakes shot

accounts outstanding
the glass is rising & falling
on 'the bones of man'
the remains of the Island

the Graveside Leek-orchid

as endangered as the memory
of my four little uncles and aunties
generations back, who never grew up
their bones buried at Campbell Town
taken in succession, by a pestilence
flowering one day, mown the next

monoculture
outside the graveyard gate
I think of all this, driving by
a neat carpet of irrigated canola
in full flower. in morning amber light
a crop duster skilfully manoeuvres his craft
low and slow on the near horizon
precision with a minimum of drift

when the roadside was diverse
unplanned leavings on the edges
the road was widened, verges disappeared
and herbicides continually mop up
old churchyards thrive on neglect
boutiques of native flora and fauna flourish
if left undisturbed, away from tidy minds

the next tiny green orchid flowering at the site
will be another amber light, to harvest rarest seed

we've mapped the place, the drought has eased
perhaps this may be the remnant year
a graveyard's story, epidemics of the past
and monocultures precious little antonym

stealth and the picturesque

The Walls of Jerusalem
picturesque in conducive weather
the uneasy language of the coloniser

crossing Fisher River
at dusk, in drizzle, on a slippery log
scent of moss and lichen — growth and decay

my footsteps sound
dull, then crunchy off track, in litter
from the forest floor, an aural exercise

indicating caution
find the quieter worn path beside
the sense of wildlife, awake in the darkness

the Trappers Hut is shelter
an overnight freeze, an early start
the plateau, sunshine reflecting on tiny tarns

then Herod's Gates
Lake Salome, Pool of Bethesda, The Temple
and other imaginings, how names excite the tourists

infiltrating ancient places
a boot impressed on a mounded cushion plant
carries the burden of a thousand years near the drama

of raw Jurassic dolerite
carved by glaciers, and alpine gardens
formed by the scraping of moraines, delicate

in the harshness
picturesque in conducive weather
the uneasy language of the coloniser

Australia Day

east coast boys
draped in flags
knotted at the neck
liquor flows
arms linked
at pace with the band
the band of brothers

hey boys
there's too much
flag waving, I say
to dribbling eyes, glazed
rootless on the 26th

in 1788 the party really started
on the 7th February when
the women disembarked
@ RSVP Sydney Cove

Arthur Philip offered
many loyal cold libations
now in public ever since
we are spinning mythology

the West

broken place

I come from a broken place. mining pillages. born into it, the alternative not apparent until I left. opaque silver-grey river not relevant. it simply was. bridges dead edged. through the eyes of a child denuded hills look natural, leaching colours configure the plastic brain. always coming home long after the family parted company with the town, the house, the street. mining pillages, but curiosity has its own reward. as a puddle dries and cracks into pushed and pulled mosaic, the edges of each fragile tesserae lift slightly, creating the shallowest depression. spaces in between expose residual moisture, release a certain aroma. I know it. mining pillages. the catchment still breathes, in the foothills.

coast to open cut - drawing like a child

bamboo paper forgives
punished with Pitt pastels
rich with pigment
working over impressions
created from the mould
paper doesn't need
a satisfying synonym

this is a memory
starting with the poem —
the all-over underlayer —
writ in fine hard graphite

line meanders on a slight diagonal
slightly right to left, on the road
year after year
coast to mountains
mountains to coast
the body of Bass Strait
separates and intrudes, into mouths —
the Mersey, the Leven, the Cam —
named for England

insert symbols of industry
a windmill
stacks from factories
finger posts along the way

pencil scratches
like keys from a real map

at the bottom, on the paper
cruelly cramped streets
battered hills, landmarks
tumble higgledy-piggledy
around a wound
an open cut
where a mountain
once embraced
a valley

Middle-earth palimpsest
below drawing, poetics
smudged, rubbed
sepia
breaking
cartographers'
hearts

catchment

gathered from trickles in the foothills
of Mount Strahan and Sorell
in and out of season water cascades
off ridges, into gullies
onto button grass and tangled tea tree
bogged and pooled from upstream torrents —
Bradden River takes effort on the human end

the rapid flowing fingerlings
rise from mist, rain, frost
overflow into the wider valley
to sea level at the shallow tided Bay

lesser known, historically exploited
logged around, tracked, burned
eaten out. blackfish, eels
crayfish, black swans
game in the playground of
colonial masters

behind Philips Island —
the convict garden —
wade to the shallow beach
black jetty remnants
reflected on tidal laps
depending on the light

upstream from the mouth
the land around regrown
a few times most likely

in the passing
of my forebears
felling, fishing, farming
in and around the hut
there was commerce
potatoes, bread, honey mead
fed by this recovering catchment

night sky reflects
across the Bay
according to the moon cycle
the season, the weather
Space X and
whatever comes next

Queenstown via the lakes

on a whim I hang a left
along Pateena Road
and ride Romantically
a horseless carriage
beside the paddocks
of the squattocracy
      a bird in a Barina
      crossing the Norfolk Plains

two whistling kites work the verges
small mammals slip under the Great Western Tiers
      emus were plentiful here before the colony
      the rats and ranks took the eggs
      museums took a pelt or two

      counter intuitively
      am I heading SSE not SSW
      then another dogleg

crisping into summer
trappings of rural engineering
fences, dams, irrigation technology
make patterns with roads, crops, buildings

Poatina pipeline is the biggest
a gash down the Tiers
power lines feed from turbines
and the station

reality is nothing
like the flow charts
illustrating the schemes

ascending now
sweat hangs on
histories hairpins
the road is virtually empty
an occasional car
a log truck now and then

someone stencilled
two white stylised
unsolicited rabbits
on a corner rockface

in the high country
wildflowers and weeds
are blooming
flies hover over fresh meat
forest ravens lift the carrion
bonsaied trees endured last season's fires
then a cider gum graveyard
near the woolshed at Miena
that shed has good acoustics
a symphony orchestra played there once

before the Ouse River bridge
an insect swarm splats the windscreen

at Bronte Park
sanitising for ice cream
the shop is full of waders
and other fishing paraphernalia
the road is sealed now
all the way to the Lyell Highway

rivers, mountains, grasses, sedges, trees
from the map and where I've been before —
The Walls of Jerusalem, the National Park —
everything delicate, vulnerable
connected, small and close

I stop to pee
listening for scant traffic
tree lines are trains
moving by deception beside the road
the ranges are stations in the distance

well past Derwent Bridge
Frenchman's Cap rises
it shines, breathes, and disappears
that mountain is a quartzite sentinel

the road becomes damp and dark
around Mount Arrowsmith, winding to the lake
thank the blockades for the Franklin River
but Lake Burbury drowned the King valley
I am mourning the old lost crossing
the Company picnic
Dad double clutching us
on a bus in 1962

around the remains of the town of Linda
Mt Owen's violent folds, alive in this light

mine workings around Mount Lyell
are thrillingly brutal

leached exposed corners
on the descent past the Iron Blow
around roadside cuttings
held back by industrial scale wire fascinators
bolted to the faces, catch falling rocks
the creek below is Conglomerate, like today

The Company is the Mount Lyell Mining and Railway Company.

how to know a Queen

the Queen flowed and flows
through my heartland
little tannin creeks fed
into thick grey water
on to the confluence with the King

tailings, heavy metal
topsoil metres deep, set solid
on the way into
and in The Bay
    the mouth is an
    underwater formation
    a drone view of the drain
    a delta shaped metaphor

one day the water changed to orange
the acid spent river accepted, as is

we will not see or know
the first custodians country
or the diarists world
in the remote Queen Valley
gigantic trees, ferns
described below the peaks

fortune seekers came
privy to the bounty

for the sake of space to heap the slag
created in the smelting, company men
diverted the course
miners dredged for gold

burning, relocation
the banks have been shored
against erosion and flooding
a river bridged toward gullies
filled with nested damp houses

a time lapse dichotomy
in requiem, to write
and care, go on
for the grit in the hills
the shingle in the river
the point of entry
the point of exit
the whole stricken system
owns the past

to own the future
know we are related
and still must come home
to compensate and advocate
the hardest close connection

the road in

driving in this afternoon
from the Strahan side
to Penghana, now
half buried under the slag heap
see the expanse of the mine
and know why all the roadside cuttings
exposing the geological layers
impress me

I drove around all the places
before dark, Batchelor Street
Orr Street, Peter Street
the sight of the old house

Latham Street, the Sand Hill
down South, Grafton Street
the graveyard and the tip

a returned soldier
foraged there when I was a girl
going to the tip was a family affair
we saw him scurrying there sometimes

for years he had a little humpy
somewhere in the hills around the town

it isn't the same
but that character Oriel in *Cloudstreet*
moved outside to a tent one day
no one said anything
    fact and fiction
    war and peace

the fetid piles and obvious rats
are gone, replaced by a refuse station

I continued on, and up Mt Jukes
just to see and feel the weather
and the ranges, knowing
every compass point

from somewhere else

pretty purple
Rhododendron ponticum
in the gardens of the town
escapee near the orange river
spreading seed
rooting deep
excreting more acid
you suckering grub
taking these hills
that barely see the sun

transport history

my family came here
to this mining town
somehow, over a century ago
a minute sliver in geological time

I came to this museum to learn
how they got there
literally, how rough the road
and the mode

before most throughfares
mines formed satellites
connected by railways

after WWI, skilled in the art
of transport engineering
on the back of the war machine
the world was changing
uncles and cousins had died knowing

the tentacles of production line
T Model Fords and Dodge Fours
bashed through and bogged
in the high country and bush

horses, bullocks, carts and drays
jockeyed with cars, trucks
Indian and Harley bikes
making new lines on maps

a street in the south of this town
is built on a swamp by the river, filled
with mangled Company trucks
dumped and dressed in soil and clay

where is the Euclid
my father embedded
near the crusher, leaping out
to save himself

where is the motor bike
abandoned on the way to Strahan
or great grandfather's Citroen
that boiled across the high country
stopping for water at every creek

what happened to the Fargo truck
Dad used for wood hooking —
lying somewhere in the bush

all the personal and Company trash
recycled into
unimaginable geological futures
or melting in the caustic river-bed

the imprinted industrial past
where they laboured
worked on the assumption
that the road was endless
and the world
a continuous bounty

cobalt blues

Mum collected the willow pattern
I've got a thing for blue and white pottery
on a tin white glaze, the blue is made
from the trace metal cobalt

I'd like to go to the potteries
in Staffordshire
gaze on the gentrified remains
of a coughing spluttering wasteland
that spewed out smoke and sweat
turning out products
for the Empire's rising middle classes
the family tree has a branch there somewhere

Congolese miners, men, women
babies on their backs, slave by hand
breathing in the dust
picking out toxic cobalt
used for lithium batteries
supplying a world-wide mosaic
for our opposing thumbs

a conifer of note

my mother's family felled Huon pine
in the years of the Great Depression
my grandfather knew those trees
crafted punts, and larger boats
perceived himself a vassal
to cold, to rain and hard work
then he worked a forge at Mt Lyell

science shows the slow growing oily Huon Pine
carries answers in the growth rings
heavy metal, including mercury
was a promiscuous escapee across the ranges
a sequestered material from the mine stacks
carried by fire, wind and tide

released worldwide from many mines
here, the golden wood entraps
bioaccumulated intelligence
corresponding to the rate
of copper smelting at Mount Lyell
The Minamata Convention is ratified now
some future good might come from this

remember The Zombies

hatters in the 19th century
were driven mad
by the vaporous stew of felt making —
couldn't remember how they came to be
in a pauper workhouse
the lunatic asylum
or a prison —
that's what mercury does

how soon the chronical of economy
chemical manufacturing, agriculture
mining, releases who knows what
into our fragile gaseous skin
drawing every breath
with the power to quieten babies
change our bodies vitals
send us somewhere instantly forgotten
it is too late to say you're sorry

    I think that was The Zombies
    on 7 QT local radio in 1964
    as pop culture zones out
    Johnny Depp gets more press
    than his Minamata movie

felting 2.0

I craft wool felt in the colours of my childhood
denuded broken yellows, pinks and greys
it took a while to work it out, there's no escape
but mine is a gentle movement, with silk hankies
stretched, distressed streaks, silver like the hills
safe and calm and mainly sane
free from that cocktail, including the protagonist

fishing the Back Channel in the punt *Maria*

I caught a ling
it sucked its way onto the bait
you laughed, and laughed
and stripped its skin
mercilessly
it was a perfect day

camp pie opened with a key
a jellied lump of lunch fell out
two sliced pieces each
you tossed the tin over the side
it's well-rotted now
like the harbour floor
all fish farms and shit

Grandad is long gone
so are the ling
it is true what you said
prescient in the '70s
your family
living rough
through the Great Depression
had the best of it

the Huon pine punt *Maria*
is on the bottom of The Harbour now
the gift of labour in its own time

extraction

Eventually we work it out. We recognise, in ourselves, our mother's hand, our father's limbs. But the mind, that is something else again. Of this one can never be sure.

Patti Smith, *Woolgathering* (2011 edition)

dear Nana

cross country from Strahan to Queenstown
riding pillion, bumped off the bike
six or seven years barren
you promptly fell pregnant

wicked

welcome home where
inside the house (occasionally even
caught, but never ever witnessed)
kids and toys and grown boys
enter the softest place and
do the thing called sacrifice

under the covers there
nothing seemed to happen
consciously, until
leaving makes sense, over time
energy makes you
see and make a world away

barker in the bushes

on the top of The Sand Hill
I met a stranger, a blind man
with his dog
I did not speak
just breath and footsteps —
afraid to say hello
I ran away

before, there were
apocalyptic sunsets
he could not see
and the sound of stones
pitched on an
old lady's roof

crawling Spion Kop and
a Plum Pudding panopticon
a boobyalla hidey hole
or cotton frottage in a shop front

Sand Hill, Spion Kop, Plum Pudding Hill: names of local landmarks
boobyalla - *Acacia longifolia*

the Dux

Janice was Dux of South Queenstown School
Fred Henry came to find a junior
with very neat handwriting
propelling her straight to the office at his Store
where the ladies drove a system
with wires
shooting tins of money and receipts
between departments
when she married
it was assumed she would be leaving
to press the Laminex of contentment

Janice was a systems-driven person
sometimes systems fail
then she went to bed clutching her babies
the confused content wrapped in
containers of fragile control

moss houses

on the south side of the house —
the cool damp side —
from the carpets of moss
growing in winter
Janice pulled up
small divots flavoured with
the earth the moss created
placing the pieces
in lumpy lines
on the sunny path
on the north side of the house

here was the bedroom
here was the kitchen
here was the front room
the perfect moss house
where seedless sponges
become final drafts

aspirational sporophytes
from impoverished moss
satisfied the dreamer
she thought about a nest
a nursery that shrivelled over time
in the sunlight

not knowing you liked green

or that you are here with Ada
this plot a memory
your emotional bone
you said your mother's rings are in there
I say how can you trust the undertaker

I ignore the shock of the green plaque
mentally caress the old granite headstone
lichen coats the epitaph
I told my sister about green
apparently green was your favourite colour
she didn't know you liked green

next time I see the plaque deliberately
surrounded by pebbles
dominating Ada's fading details
mother of you

I think about green plants
with coloured flowers
all weeping in bloom
you wept at sad movies
weeping over and over
in a bed of confusion
I wept like a child
as a child
until it stopped
until this green reaper

anecdotally comparing my mother to Kerry Packer

my mother had a lot of confused guilt; debilitating, secretive, obsessive, lonely in a way, she had very few friends. Kerry Packer had a lonely childhood, suffering from polio and absent parents. a heavy gambler later, he handed large amounts of cash to croupiers and 'friends'. Mum surrounded herself with chocolate chip biscuits, trashy magazines, VHS videos and stuff in boxes. Packer's father started the *Women's Weekly*. Mum subscribed every week until it became a monthly, then she got the monthly, long after her own ended. Packer had a code name in the press, Goanna. Mum worried a goanna poking it with a stick to amuse herself, she said look at it, look at it. the goanna, on its haunches, hissed back. after a car crash when he was young, Packer gave up alcohol. Mum did not drink when she was young and took home brew secretly through the night when she was older, maybe until she died. I don't know. they both suffered from ill health for years. he managed to secure a kidney, but she couldn't afford health insurance and always waited on a list; she didn't need a kidney, just other things. to toughen the fuck up, Kerry placed his son James with the now disgraced 'Chainsaw' Dunlap, author of *Mean Business*. Jamie became James. Mum became Janice and stood at the door, saying I don't want to have anything to do with my children, they are an inconvenience, and my grandchildren are a complication. the compliment, 'emotionless', Kerry said in admiration of Dunlap. exclusion has a cruel agency, said the witness.

In Tasmania it is common to call a blue tongue lizard a goanna.

a viewing

the shower ran hot
Veronica took the call
and knocked
on the bathroom door
I took my time
towelled off

it was my birthday
we went out as planned
next day I drove to the coast
visiting the old haunts

Janice didn't want a funeral
a few days grew a ceremony
anyway, and we gathered
I wondered how a fragile lady
carried such power

I burned a few hand-written
pagan paper offerings
on the front porch
of the old house
trawled the photos
touched the cold hands
felt the energy of grief
in the room
around the casket

it had been at least
a decade since we met

how tiny the remains
little messages left
resting, tied with ribbon
a few Mills & Boon
to take into the furnace

learnings and leanings

I owe you mother, not on a slate
but gratitude, without a seatbelt
tossed around in the Vanguard
past Yolla, past the last red soil and farms
knowing you will say every vista out loud

pulling in at Hellyer River
after a wide-eyed winding drive
overhung with the first myrtles
we wander, like sucklings
down the child sized track

you know about petrified wood
we stop at the fractured green log
it seems too precious to touch
it's the way you said it

running water is music through the trees
the sodden soil soft and slippery
releases a scent I can't describe
then the river, with all its strength
coming from nowhere, going somewhere

for all that happened later
all the fragility, the unknown
you took that time and gave it
confident in place, petrified inside
but enough for me to feel it, always

pioneer museum

indulge the memories
all aspects of a kid's life
in a mining town
late 50's early 60's
the hospital baby crib
that I must have laid in

Central School
new bowl haircut
grey uniform
the plastic school bag
a Kodak Box Brownie
living in our cupboard
a spread of Happy Family cards
from the Christmas stocking

massive projectors from the Paragon
film light illuminating all the motes
God Save the Queen
and Bambi beams out

the Little Golden Book
Babes in Toyland
a plot so convoluted
so many villains
and good guys
I've come home

progress at Grafton Street

a shed
services a family
set on wooden stumps
a square, unlined
flat roofed wash house
clad with second hand
corrugated iron

inside to the right
installed under a window
double pine wash troughs
fed by copper pipes and brass taps

dry splitting Velvet soap bars
a bleached laundry stick
hard remnants of Reckitt's Blue
in muslin bags
vintage on eBay now
sit somewhere on the sill

near the hand wound wringer
a washing machine on castors
to the left a privacy stall
a claw foot bath and a kero heater
the green bentwood chair
the creaky door with hooks
holding towels and clothes

the night cart man came by
and wandered up the yard
I was sitting on the new steps
and watched him carry
a stinking slopping can
slung on his shoulder
the truck moved up the street

that is how it was when we came back —
moving on from a tin bath by the inside fire —
watching effluent leave the premises

the ferry at the Mersey River

Janice went to Melbourne
on *The Princess* ferry
one time, with Dad
a simple overnight sailing

waiting dockside
just 13 years old
I watched the crowds
looked up and saw them both
leaning on a post

from the decks
paper streamers
fluttered down

the crew released spliced ropes
from the bollards
everyone clung to paper
weaving under
and around each other
till the last one tore

I sobbed tangled
multicoloured emotions
a web fell into the river
it seems extreme
in retrospect

the ferry turned
the horn blew
the dock emptied

they were away for one week
then Janice said
I'm never going there again

pay day

without a plan
a weekly pay packet
created opportunities
    don't mention the journey
    in context that word is so annoying

loud to quiet confusion
a house for seven reduced to one
driven from within
    there's an out of context
    line from a song
    you'll learn to love it later

it doesn't matter
here is a gem of wisdom
    a clever mouse
    has more than one hole

rebounding to Peter Street
the first crib
weeds surround
a doorless memorial
that pulses like a
perpetual radar saying
make a home from that bitch

Robbie Robertson, *Somewhere Down the Crazy River*,
song released in 1987

the leavings

I walked the concrete paths
gutters and steps just as it was
the house long gone

in the remains
I picked up the hardened leather tongue
from a child's shoe

see the cold bedrooms
paisley eiderdowns
fresh bread and fat
kitchen kerosene fumes
and stained walls

silkie hens, budgies
a dismembered frog sacrificed
running through new pipes
flowing for the first time

lino, grey and yellow Laminex
I cannot let the colours be
doors, windows, weather
spicy nasturtiums
in shaded places
fresh cut bush wood
baby powder
on the bathroom floor

the deconstructed leavings
stacked inside a shed
the value of materials —
bricks, burnie board
4x2s, tins of nails
sheets of corrugated iron —
the container of the container
of my earliest memories

becoming a dowser

on a summer day at Mount Pleasant
in the middle of a long paddock
my father took instruction
arm tops tucked close to the side
forearms horizontal, extending
rods, a couple of sticks, twisting
in the hands till the bark broke
free, his head thrust back
mouth wide laughing, unexpected
divination with no effort whatsoever
dowsed with that erection
till the fluid flowed, his power
smashed the paradigm that
hard work guarantees success

no satisfaction

at the roundabout I always turned at Palmers Road —
that day I came to help
the chainsaw belted out bitter rounds of macrocarpa

vapour made a pig, a dog
in retaliation for service
to your broken body

spewing out, the logs
were rolled and lifted
but not to your satisfaction

the splitter split
enzymes were released
around the roundabout

the urge to turn
at Palmers Road
abated by perspective

post combustion from the rounds
time passes. the sting melts
setting solid sometimes though —
when it is cold enough

aged

sitting here near your bed
waiting for the infusion
and the cardiac team
in the queue, stamped aged
since August last
I can see the frustration
tiredness in your long night
knowing it is accelerating

we need to do something
preferably with corrugated iron
with something you collected
and stored, something useful
something that is a memory
of how fit you once were
filled with generative power
charged with particles of energy
to overlay on the broken bits

cut it up with tin snips
make new parts
a heart, kidneys, eyes
backbone, hips
your body bouncing
into action like your mind

you can hear a baby crying
in a cubicle across the way
it worries you

considering your deafness
you are constantly aware of
charging your phone

you mentioned the virus last night
it has curbed your excesses
your love lives a little way across town
you can't see each other very much

when you got out of Nasho in '57
you said *I'll never line up again*
and here I am still lining up

iron is going in now
infused not corrugated
you have always been feisty
lately in different ways
playing the waiting game
knowing you rely on teams
and live on despite the box
they put you in

let's build another
full of all the component parts
of everything you ever made
ironically you said
I don't think I'll have another family
we'll put the one you have in that box too

at the rave

you shock me still Dad
you ordered me to
get this thing out of my snout

intensive care delirium
a circadian juggernaut
overwhelmed you

massive foam gloves
swallowed your fine motor skills
you said *I'll fight*
a big bendy fist
symbolized your last punch

you asked for me
even now I hardly believe that

what music does he like?
that was easy
singing along to Patsy Cline
you really were
walking after midnight
it wasn't pretty but you came in
on the choruses

it goes away they said
you came back
for a few days and held
a last audience for the
passing parade

becoming an orphan

the vagueness of an
might mean I stop by
and visit that graveside

imagine the flesh fallen
from that broken body
titanium wrestling with bones

that held you together
you didn't fancy a cremation
so there you are

on every drive by
until that graveyard
gets re-purposed

in the future
it isn't easy being
orphaned

you are an idea
a plot a form
of immunity

Dad's mother, Nana Dulcie's sister, 'Baby' had a stroke

after Baby's stroke
the doctor said, you're next
unless that weight comes off

Dulcie started eating
like a budgie, wasting away
never sitting at the table

when we visited, before
or after that wake-up call, my Nana
always leaned against the kitchen cupboard

while the family tucked in hard and fast
big meals, sponges covered in fruit and cream
the old girl, it was said, made a good plum pudding

the kitchen was the gathering place
in every house, over so many moves
ten splintered births, over generations

that's what I remember most, her separate life
cooking, washing dishes, splitting sticks, lighting fires
clearing ash and painting the hearth with ochre

silent and saggy, living
on the edge, Dulcie lived inside
until the day she died

Mum's sister in a coma

I

I'm thinking about Latham Street
behind the hospital, butted
on the frosty south-west side
of the Sand Hill where my
little cousin died, accidentally
playing outside, I'm thinking

about your brother swilling
beer, Camel smokes, pub
corner doors, walking past
rancid air, murmuring by
open summer windows
'down the street'

a classic deco butcher
hanging beasts become
corned beef, mashed potatoes
parsley sauce, carrots and
broad beans at her table

II

back in '66 with my sister
we wait it out there
and learn, with Mum in
Devonport maternity
we have another sister

Dad's at home, every day
he walks past the cage
at the back door, where
our budgies starved to death
on their backs, legs in the air
like Mum giving birth
he loves all animals
but she's the one that fed them

III
I'm thinking about my aunt
so distant for decades, being
your sister, I'm thinking
it's lucky she survived
and went home to the West
and how I felt ringing her number
and taking that step

Emma May runs away

burning up at Sassafras would be a blur
a virus memory, heavy as the illness
that left you deaf
Mrs Savage locked the woodshed
for a week, food and water
passed under the door
the fever fevered
and weakened

you ran away to Devonport
living on the streets and
became a little housemaid for a vicar
Victor came with his hand
his future determined your future
you moved to Strahan
I've been on the road today
wondering how you travelled
it was rough then, just a track

the men were fishing, pining
growing vegetables with you on Philips Island
you baked, kept bees, made mead
through the years of the Great Depression

fresh and free
camping at The Bay
good for your girls
my great aunties

they left a carefree record
perching on the punt
dipping in the water
walking the beach
at Braddon River
taking lessons outside
in the sun, with Horace
their dear brother
my grandfather

if sight and sound
could fill a wound
that must be it

Emma May's embrace

the shock of your warmth
the kindness in your eyes
the smell of ginger cake
the quiet
and the ticking of the clock

the fountain and the lake

apparently we are cardinal.
like a bird or a boss
according to the predictors of the stars

I am water, you are water
you are intuitive, you sting
according to the predictors

I am supposed to be a homemaker
but you are domestic, like a weapon
with a dishwasher
I am still in therapy dealing
with the hoarding
      this makes no sense

I might be about *the moon* on the water
I may have born you, the fountain
your energy disturbing the surface

we are both all about the feels
when sad things happen
when bad things happen
even in movies
or when sirens wail
we wail

sunset

we reach the crest
a valley opens
facing west
streaks of apricot
cross the sky
ripening, riper
I say it is glorious
you say
I want to change my name
to Glorious

the bowl fills
seed spills
in sanguine broth

notes from the 14th November 2019
a day in labour

Veronica is labouring now
this café is distracting
James is on the way
they want to meet their baby girl

Piazzo San Marco flooded this week
waters broken this morning
with mitigation on some lips
and denial on others
ours are plump, to plant kisses

trust without evidence, or
a matter for the law —
Vera May
entrusted to us
you are here
hope fills
the minutes of every day

the baby

Vera's ear embossed your skin
as she rested in your arms
you met her crying, perfect
and cried your blues in a few days
rocking automatically

house of milk

pumping like a cow
reporting to authority
evidence is in
the babe is flourishing
the cat has nibbled a nipple shield
he's acting out
he wants your product
no one predicted this

mondegreens at three

it's six in the evening
the sunsets contracting
we've been out for sushi
then off to the playground
made a river with a water rill
manufactured mud pies
set up a shop
and flogged off the lot

it's 2023 you are still
officially three
we rinse off our hands
race to the car

you request
your playlist
it's OutKast
you sing along
in mondegreens
Roses got rhyme
rhythm, repetition
'roses really smell
like poo-poo-ooh '
that bit's down pat
from the back seat
it is a catchy tune
we drive away
it is bath time

castings

when is a shadow not a shadow, when it's the shadow I'm showing my granddaughter so she knows what a shadow is – not the shadow of a soul, but the shadow of us, the two of us, cast on the deck as the afternoon sun pulls in behind us and throws us out, long shadows that meet our feet where we hieroglyph and dance and laugh.

types of shadows that form because of the light, crisp shadows of summer afternoons, or relaxed – like a pillow of leaves – shadows of the cosmos that make autumn, or open crescent moons, an eclipse, or the shadows of the system that have a reason, because there is a reason, even without understanding or knowing or seeing.

I didn't say all that.

happenings

the mourning dove

this is the long season
of the mourning dove
language rolls over one
millennia, to another

tumbling all
troublesome words
till agony becomes the victim
of semantic drift
numbed on screens
and I know
babies born in war
like the symbolism and fact
of the mourning dove
miss the scribe

talismans

I just hold onto sunsets
plus breathing air
that's all I've got

no North American Indian chief
kooky purple alien
or medieval baroness
guiding from my right shoulder
putting pressure on the joint

I like rocks
plopping them in plant pots
knowing where each one came from
a paddock, or a roadside

routines are hard
resistant to ceremonies
or morning rituals
but craving Tai Chi
and chi tea, every day

I like to consider entropy
without understanding the physics

Film-Makers' Cinémathèque letterhead

searching on-line through the
National Gallery of Victoria portal
a graphic print
Cinémathèque Letterhead
by the late father of Fluxus
George Maciunus
induced the laws of physics
sucked me into a wormhole
I was drawn to the film strip image
with text for sprockets
not pretty, expansive
or blockbuster worthy
the rest is simply blank

Cinémathèque reminds me
of the hallucinations I had
emerging from anaesthesia
my heart stopped
for thirty seconds
paddled three times
and surreal film strips
recorded all the action
my strips were very busy

Maciunus was too
accounts of his behaviour
remind me of my father
— in some ways —

staring down authority
belligerent
aggressive
charming

Cinémathèque is the culprit
Fluxus, the movement
the Manifesto
happenings
assemblages
the New York avant-garde
John Cage

Maciunus was committed
against critics
dilettantes and professionals
he engaged and enraged
while he lived
no signatures
no ownership
anything can be art
anyone can do it

Gilbert & George weighed in
as human sculptures in the early years —
there is a photo in the collection —
their gold glittered selves
in suits, dancing and singing
that good old pub song
about homelessness
underneath the arches

MONA's huge retrospective
was a blockbuster
I loved their more than upwardly mobile
oversized body fluid art
two men one artist visited Tasmania
and flogged a lot of product

Yoko Ono worked with Maciunis
I thought about the Happenings
the bed-ins, John Lennon gunned down —
in the other arches in the foyer of the Dakota —
like so many leaders calling out for peace

Cinémathèque is the culprit
Macuinus ate my homework
Gilbert and George vlogged
their lockdown exile

my brain holds the memory of
a ketamine-induced surreal film clip
archived in my private collection

arteries

...there are places even within ... a modern metropolitan sprawl where the boundaries between past and present, wild and domestic, collapse together.

Simon Schama,
Landscape and Memory,
p 577

The Tailrace – diverted water

beside a long dual carriageway, and a sub-station
in the suburbs, by the Tamar River estuary
a busy children's playground, bbqs, car parks

I sit by the inlet and hear four bird languages
five, six, seven, eight and more
dampening the sound of humming traffic

a fur seal grips a big silver fish
in its mouth, slapping it on the water
a minute ago, the seal was languid
turning slowly, spraying water
fore flippers gently turning up
hind flippers stirring, in the bath

a mass of seagulls
flock up on a chance
squark into seal business
around and around
'til the director's cut

another seal appears from the shallows
swims across, responding to the commotion
both seals disappear under water
one comes back and flops onto the blue jetty
fodder for the paparazzi —
dog walkers, kayakers —
the creature owns the space

the tide eases out, sucking reflections
from grey clouds, and intermittent blue sky

invading willows on the banks of the race
drop bright yellow leaves in the breeze

today I learned to identify a juvenile Pacific gull
seeking to name, seeking to know
penstocks divert, turbines crush —
the parkland eats away
beside protein enriched soup —
birds quieten, but for one predatory raven

the traffic is taking over now

the eco echo of a recreational garden: The Basin

the unreconciled lake
weirs, bridges, the dam
pathways inserted in the 19th century
floods come and leave tumbled woody parts
smooth whole dead trees deposited
in windrows on manicured lawns

exotics — deciduous, evergreen pines
a bank of rhododendrons, the daffodil walk —
wattles, dogwood, blanket leaf
persist in the middle storey
giving way to a few black peppermint

swans, ducks, all types of wild fowl
were noted by the colonials
silver eyes, scrub tits
and New-Holland honeyeaters
meet you on the pathways
white herons pick off elvers
working over rocks against the current

sheoaks find some purchase
in humus-filled cracks
water freezes, ice swells
dolerite boulders shear off
up and down into the river
along the sublime pathways

by the end of the swimming season
pool side, above The Basin proper
scent of chlorine dominates the lawn
water is at risk

upstream lifestyle homes
with great granite kitchens
hug the mass of water above the dam
excreting in every way, poisoning weeds
and further back farmers fertilize
seasons of algal bloom

a flock of seagulls
flew around the pool and lake
in a figure of eight, twice circled
mesmerising a summer evening crowd
standing waist deep, quieted, gazing up
underbelly feathers, reflected
unnaturally blue
and nothing happened
a whip snake slithered away
from all the customers
back into the rocks

Prince's Square

when the water was turned on and the oak trees were saplings
eucalypts, were still ringbarked on the edges of a small town
fires burned in windrows, and watercourses were engineered
on Palawa country

a brickfield became a rubbish dump, a parade ground
a site for public hangings
parkland happened
around a bronze fountain
rumour has it the piece was sent in error
and never returned to the Northern Hemisphere

common in our parkland
rows of acanthus from Corinthian antiquity
riddled with the symbolism of mortality like a Grecian urn
or resurrection and everlasting life on a de Medici tomb
rhizomes eat into Princes clay

Neptune, Galatea, Amphitrite and Acis
are castings poured in France
occupying the central fountain
the water god and goddesses of Ancient Greece
patrolled by goldfish, in a lily pond

gargoyles with fishy lips
deliver water
four chubby nymphs
circle the fountain waist
rushes sprout from the top
at night it is all theatre
Romance and flood lights

I've had rugs and picnics
a baby in a stroller
I've passed through, looked up
enjoyed a hawthorn's haws above a park bench
I've chained daisies, stopped to like lichen
and seasonal moss, admired the south side
of sequoias, velvet in winter
I've observed spring weddings
leaf-blowers, sucking out the crunch

crowds mourn, celebrate
rage even, listen to music, dance
march out into the streets
for the water and the future

the journey of the longfin and shortfin eel

years ago, I caught a longfin eel
around a lot of rocks and weed
the line bent, as it circled
pulling on the hook and bait
people gathered, impressed
it was so fat and long, the eel
landed in a net and met its end
fated to be soused for the dinner table

I did not know the eel story then
it really is a cycle, in the waters
off the Tropic of Capricorn
billions of eel spawn
swept through thousands of kilometres
of salt water to this island
swept home by currents
to familiar

eels live long —
25, 35, 50 years
depending on the species —
in waterways and dams

when the time is right
migration is immanent
then spawning and death
somewhere in the Coral Sea
and other seas
at least that is what the scientists
are trying to prove

an incomprehensible code
creates millions
of leaf shaped larvae

on our continental shelf
a metamorphosis
larvae elongate into transparent glass
then take colour from the places
where briny becomes brackish
then fresh, in estuaries
rivers, streams and dams

eels keep it tidy
eating up their world
slithering over land
between water holes
burrowing into mud
sometimes even forming
an eel wheel, rotating
together to cross an obstacle

elvers find little cracks
in dam walls, the eel
takes everything we throw at it
loss of habitat, harvesting
micro-plastic pollution
some are crushed in turbines

this fish prefers a nocturnal
and mysterious life
my eel had lived long
I am sorry it was where it was
hiding, opportunistic
cleaning up the meat on that line

high country encounter

unsealed, the Marlborough Highway
cuts across the high country
crosses the upper reaches
of the Ouse River
by dammed watercourses
salmonid fisheries
hydroelectricity penstocks
a village in a valley

above that village before
really solid infrastructure
a wedge-tailed eagle stares down
the little car, standing over carrion
       – roadkill, not a lamb –
       another miscarriage of justice
       the perceived enemy prefers
       mopping up and hunting rabbits
       the scourge of Australian farms

at a standstill
from a distance
I waited
the eagle awaited
its own assessment
stood erect, spread wings
lifted off with agency
muscle, lightness of bone
length of span, and feathers
up and over the farm fence

to a eucalypt branch
perched then watched the road

the slip stream was palpable
hearable, almost viewable
I drove by slowly
reverent

look away, there's nothing
leverageable, not an image
to the cloud, not a cloud this day
just rippling heat and blue sky

Note: The Marlborough Highway and Ouse River, Tasmania

searching for the Miena cider gum

at the Miena Backpackers
it was 3:24 am in this diary
fully clothed in bed wearing a beanie
this was a two-doona night

I had come to see trees
half bare of leaves
some grown for hundreds of years

the endangered sub species
Miena Cider Gum
needs cold frosty places
when the sap rises in summer it leaks
over millenniums
the boozy drink has been tapped

I had wandered the day before
through light snow
at a roadside stand of three gums
one was sawn, a limb on the ground
another half fallen. it was grey overhead
the trees glazed by rain

grazing deer and cattle
had stripped the bark
colours were intense
greens, yellows, apricots
bleeding out

I used my phone
to record the sight —
imagine the outcry
if I had captured murder
as it happened

then it was 8.30 am
too cold to shower
it was hostile
at the truck stop
uhf frequency sent an occasional blurt
the one Kenworth outside
loaded with colossal windfarm parts
waiting for the snow plough
had pulled in close to five am

I strung out a cup of tea
to stay warm, but
there wasn't much time
I wanted to talk to someone
about three Miena cider gums

negative ions

on the ground by waterfalls and waves
the wind from the Southern Ocean —
tightening flesh around bones —
enough to inhale invisible charges

after storms with lightning —
a tasty post-intimate polarization

Sloop Rock rollers
on the West Coast
are strong
gazing to that mass
I felt visceral lust
questioning Romance
and Science

powerful movement,
a threatened forest of kelp
slapping below the surface
saline spritzers
rising from below

walking back
from ocean
to the harbour
dry grass rattled
in the heat
beneath my stride
a tiger snake at 45 degrees
quietly chilled my spine
I walked on
turbulent to calm

Patti Smith and the bird

when all this is over I want to see the life ahead
with oxygen, and four clear seasons
at the 40th parallel, reassuring all the other latitudes
so the Short Tailed Shearwater can still migrate every year

I intend to write each day and almost do
like Patti Smith, journaling without fear, always sure,
sitting at her café table breaking bread to dip in oil and vinegar
still reading Baudelaire, and I, like a fan girl, know
she sings, people have the power, as the light in the sky
is fuelled by carbon, generating stunning sunsets and sunrises

I want to dream again about my father, calling out *help* for the first time
incomprehensible, as Patti wrote about the half-finished tracts
my sheets of crumpled paper, scraps on napkins, lost between lofts
sitting on my stoop, watching and waiting for the birds to return

Notes

dancing in dirt, *quote* ref. 'matter out of place' anthropologist and cultural theorist Mary Douglas, author of *Purity and danger: An Analysis of Concepts of Pollution and Taboo*, 1966.

stealth and the picturesque The Walls of Jerusalem is an alpine park situated in the Tasmanian Wilderness World Heritage Area.

the road in This poem references Oriel Lamb, a character in Tim Winton's novel *Cloudstreet* (1991).

cobalt blues *The Dark Side of Congo's Cobalt Rush* By Nicolas Niarchos. *The New Yorker*, May 24, 2021.

Patti Smith and the bird, 'when all this over,' words from the oft cited Irish poet, translator and editor Eiléan Ní Chuilleanáin's sonnet, *Swineherd*. Also acknowledging the memoirs of Patti Smith.

Minamata Convention on Mercury – the mercury poems p 34, 35, 36. Australia has now signed and ratified the Minamata Convention. With this responsibility it is important to identify mercury in the environment. Protecting human health and environmental impacts from mercury and mercury compound emissions are the core aims of the Convention. https://minamataconvention.org/en

Published previously

'Negative Irons' and 'Positive Outcomes' in October 20 2022, was read live during a promotional interview for the Dragline Festival in Queenstown, with Kylie Baxter on Evenings.

'The Graveside Leek-orchid' was published in *Island Magazine*, Issue 164 in 2022

Some poems have been reworked from the self published chapbook *Roughly*, from 2022.

Acknowledgements

To Ralph Wessman, Helga Jermy, Dr Deb Malor, Penelope Layland, Kristen Lang, Cameron Hindrum, Michelle O'Byrne, Emmalie Kyle, Jane Williams, Therese Corfiatis, Jenny Sayer, Nancy Jean Corbett, Nesta Hardy, Yvonne Gluyas, Joy Elizabeth, Tim Slade, Peter Still, Paul Mansfield, Jenny McKay, Kylie Clinton, and Raymond Arnold and Helena Demczuk at PressWEST, Queenstown. All have encouraged and supported my writing, through friendship, reading the manuscript, listening, and offering me space to perform, write and edit.

I would like to express my appreciation to Joanne Huxley, Tasmanian Museum and Art Gallery, Research Officer, who facilitated access to the journals of TB Moore.

In Queenstown I reconnected with my late aunt, Geraldine White (née Nielsen) and met and stayed with her when she was well. Our conversations and time together were easy and blanketed in memory, of family and The Bay. I would like to especially thank her son, my cousin, Stephen White for his support.